Coffee Time

A Coffee Lover's Coloring Book

illustrated by
Rachel Jones

Copyright © 2016, All rights reserved.

FREE BONUS PAGES

Visit: http://racheljonesarts.com/coffee-time/ to receive a PDF of 5 bonus coloring pages.

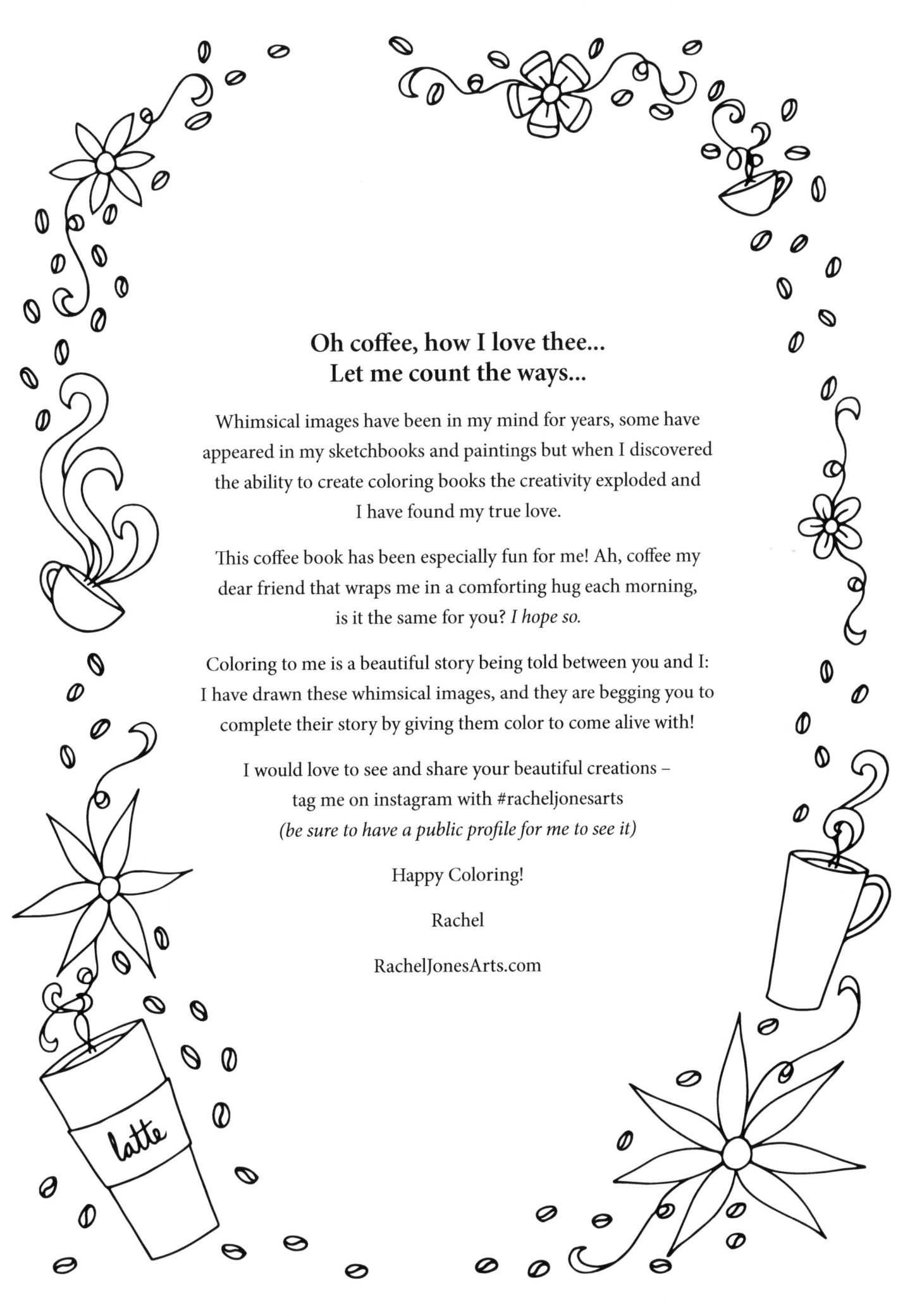

Oh coffee, how I love thee...
Let me count the ways...

Whimsical images have been in my mind for years, some have appeared in my sketchbooks and paintings but when I discovered the ability to create coloring books the creativity exploded and I have found my true love.

This coffee book has been especially fun for me! Ah, coffee my dear friend that wraps me in a comforting hug each morning, is it the same for you? *I hope so.*

Coloring to me is a beautiful story being told between you and I: I have drawn these whimsical images, and they are begging you to complete their story by giving them color to come alive with!

I would love to see and share your beautiful creations – tag me on instagram with #racheljonesarts
(be sure to have a public profile for me to see it)

Happy Coloring!

Rachel

RachelJonesArts.com

But first, Coffee.

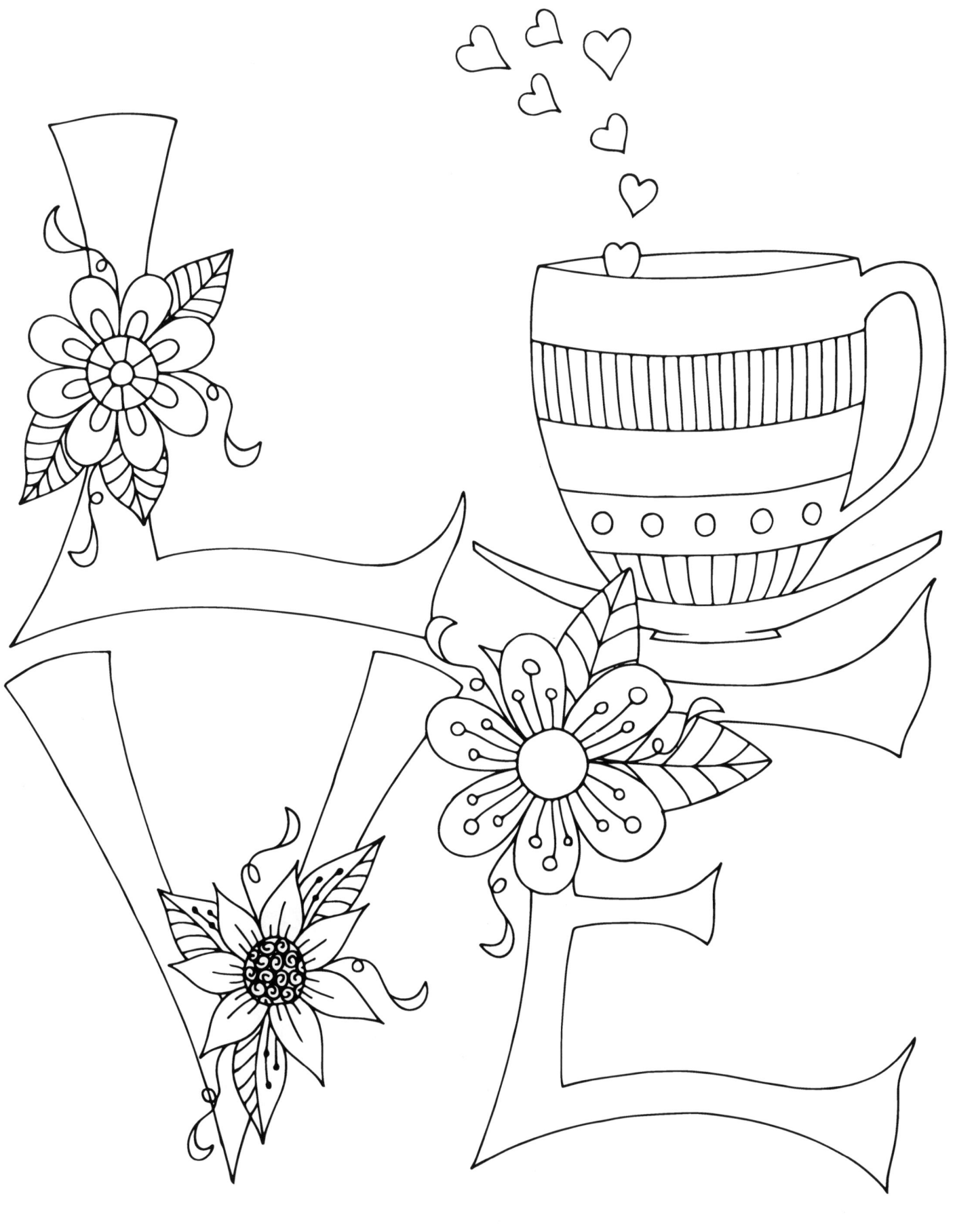

Coffee therapy

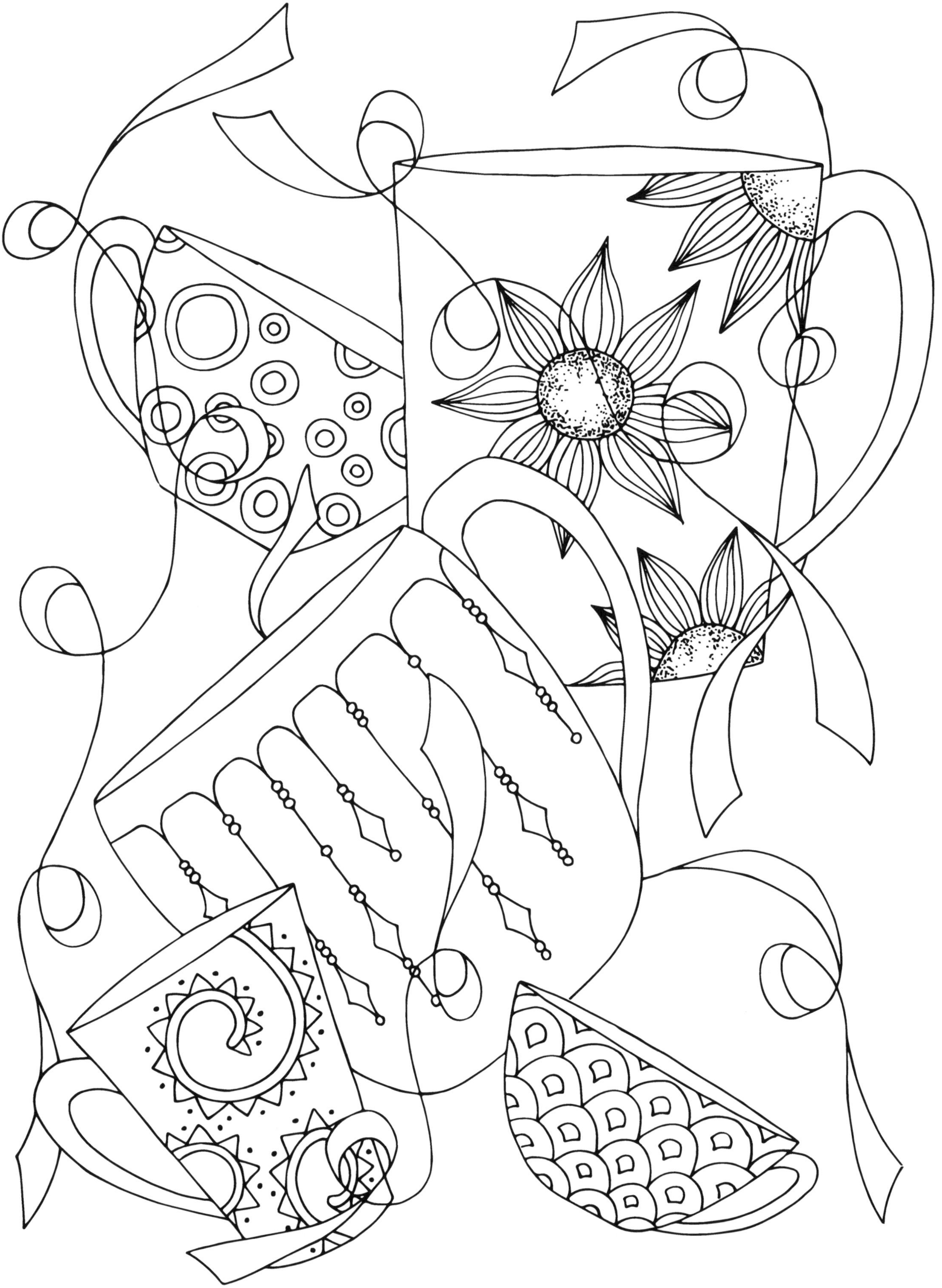

Love is in the air

And it smells like coffee

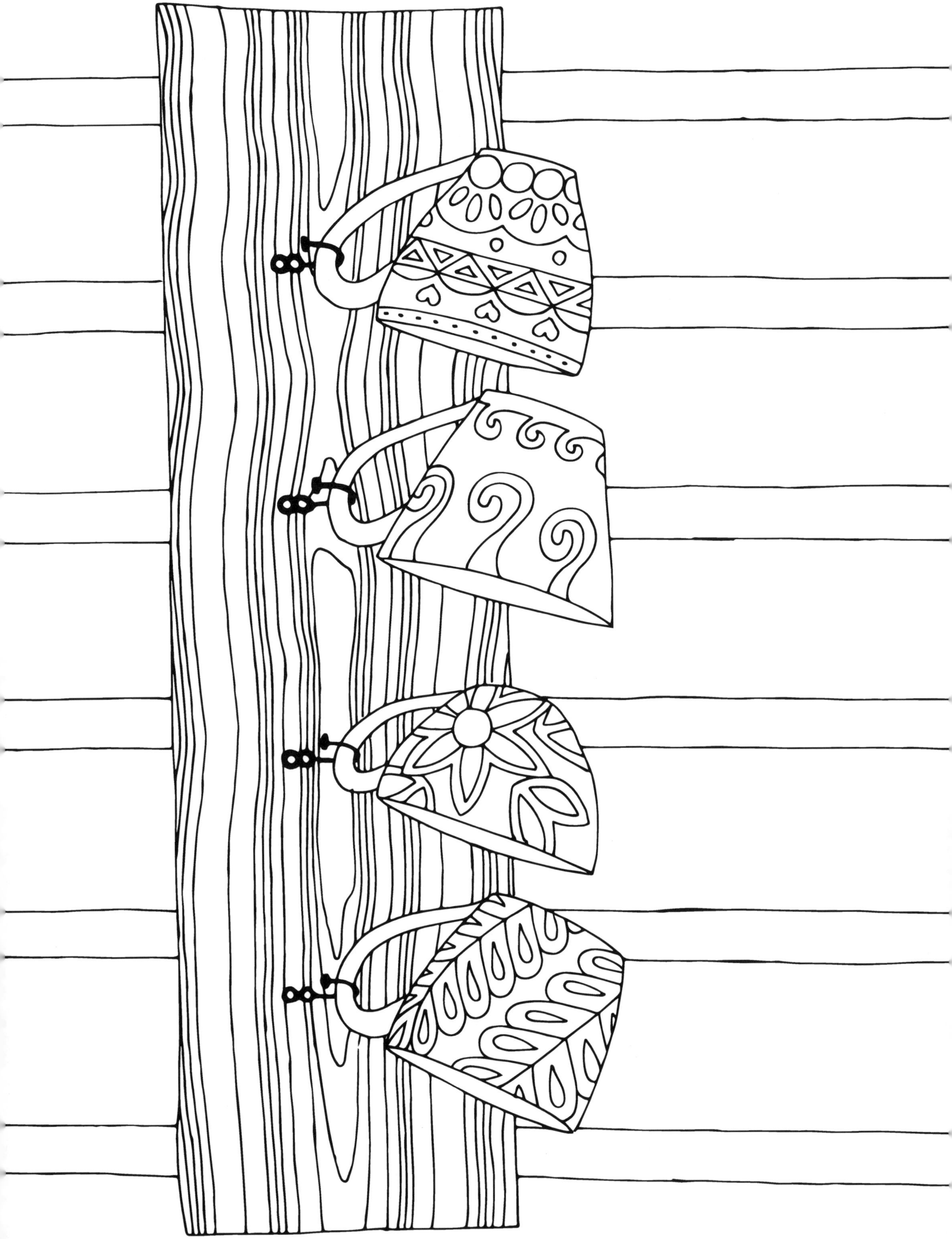

"You can do it!"

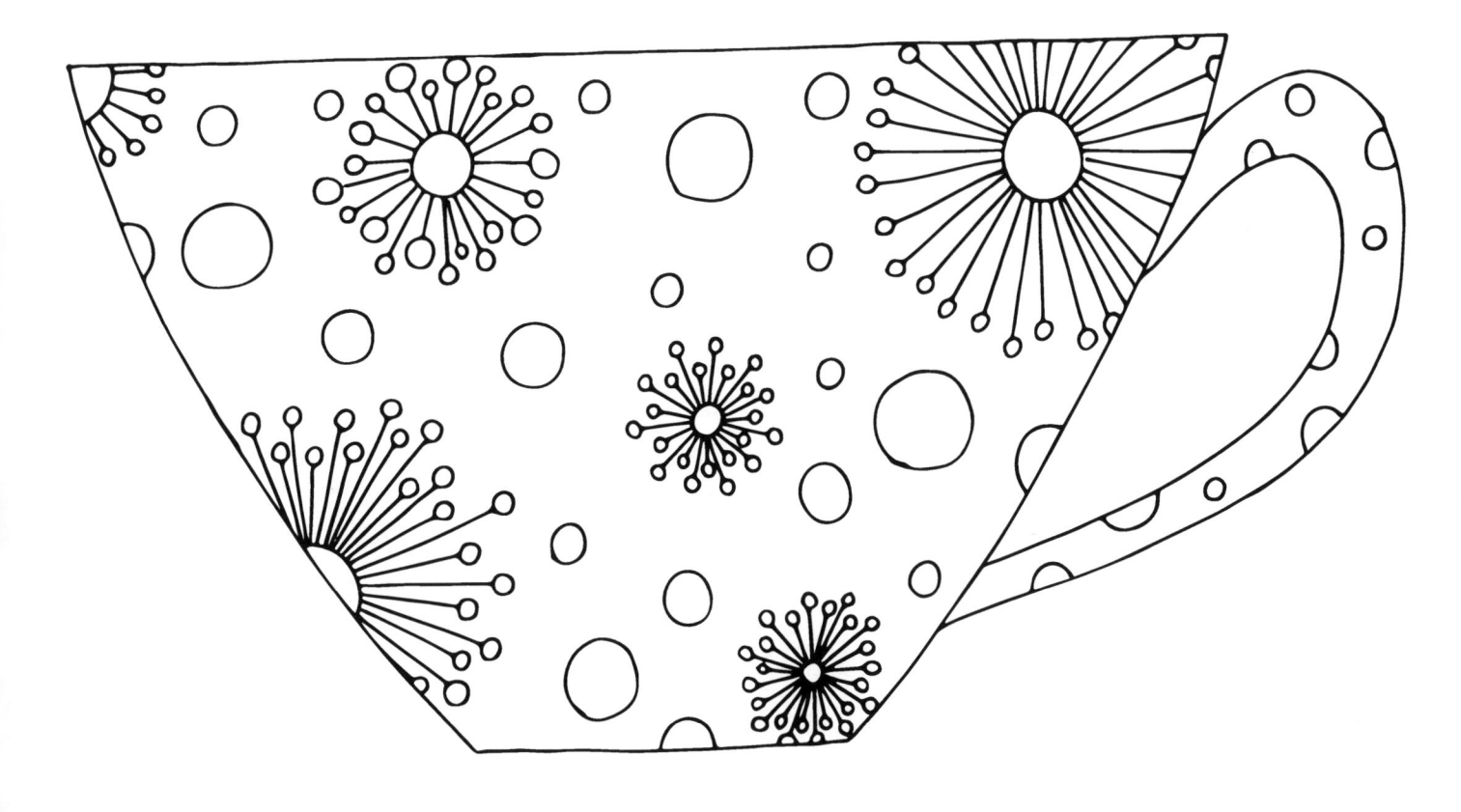

— Coffee

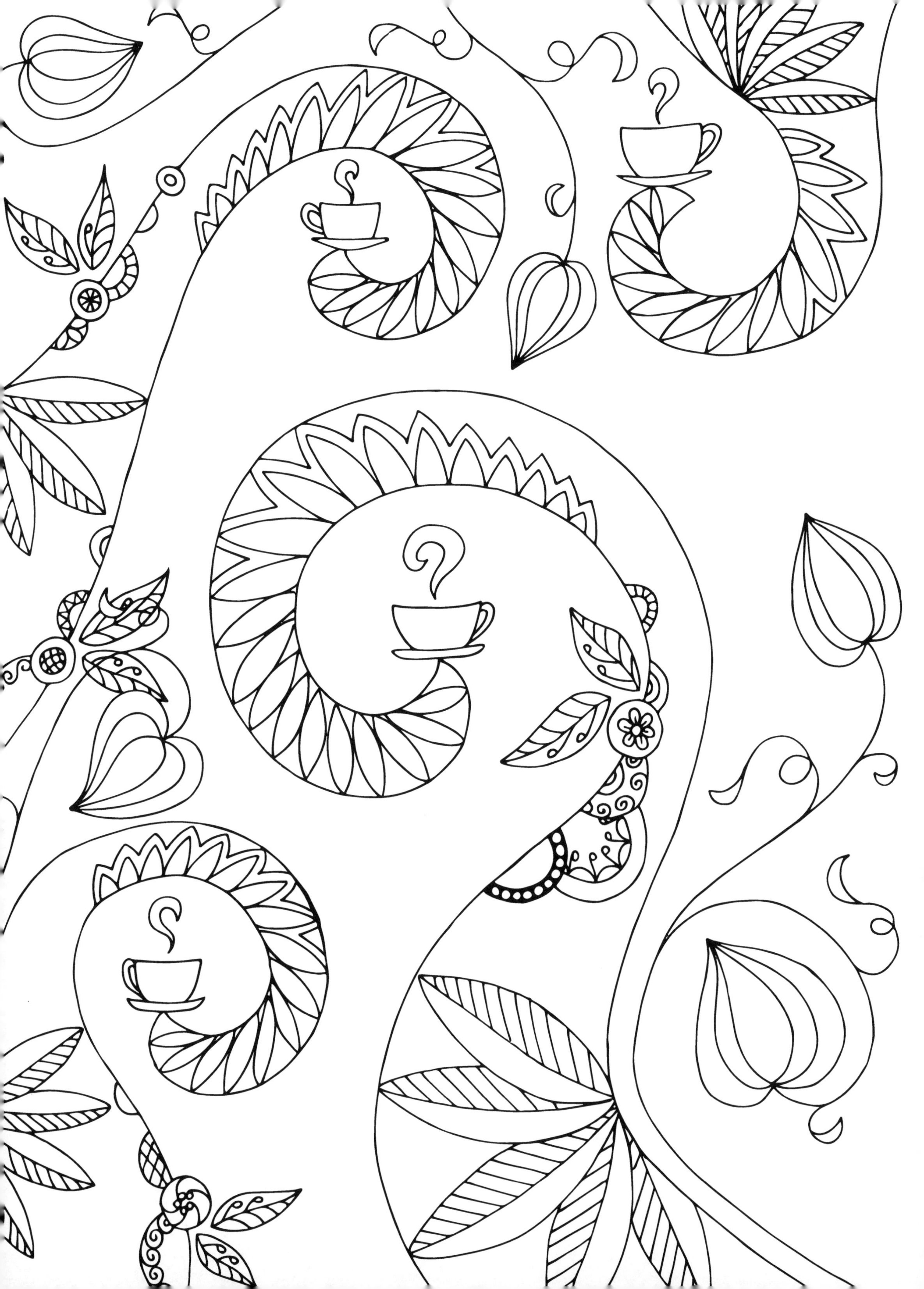

Coffee is the Elixer of Life

COFFEE TIME

First I drink the Coffee. Then I do the things.

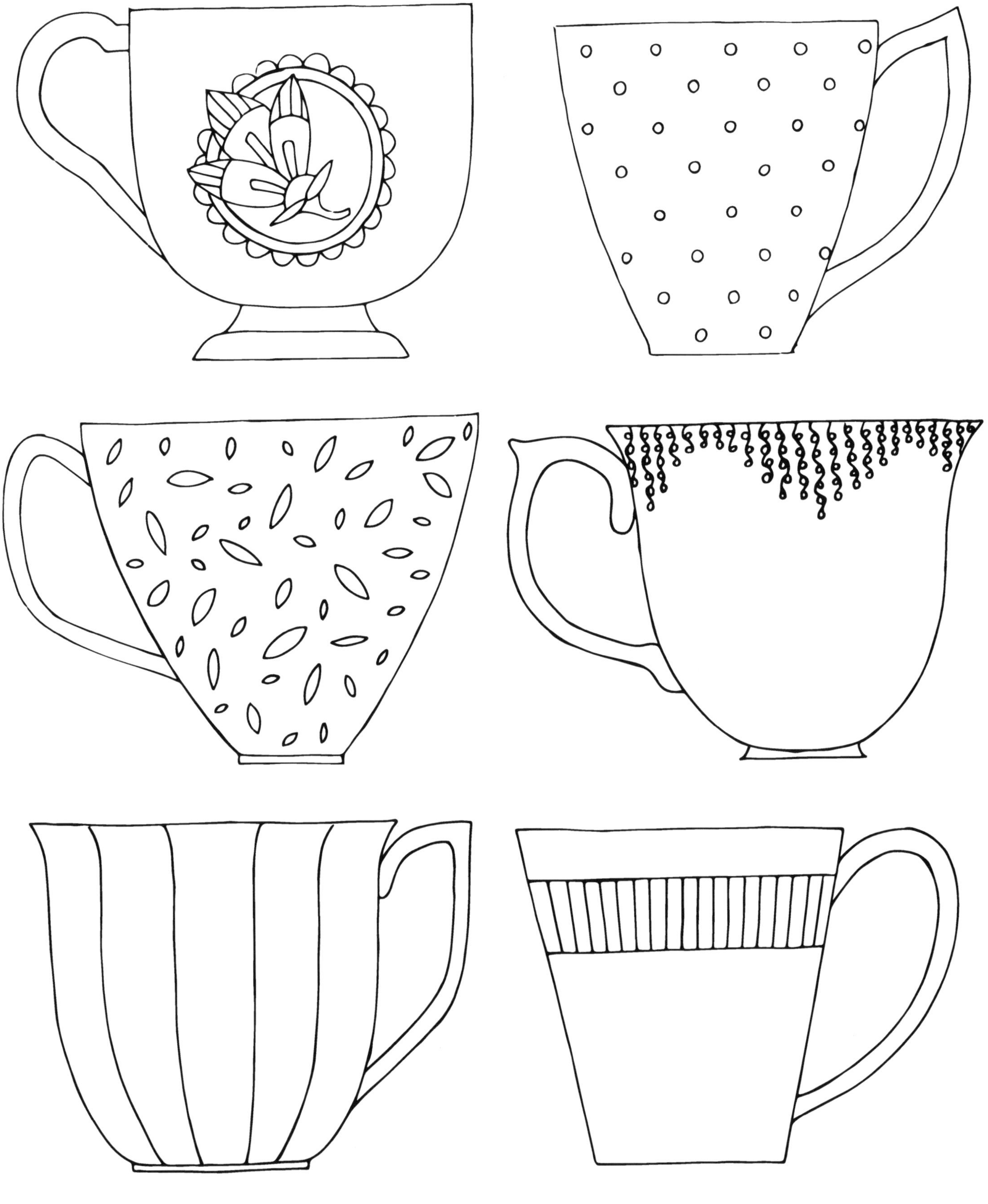

CAPPUCCINO
COFFEE
Espresso
BREVE
French Roast
COLUMBIAN
Affogato
Flat White
CAFE MOCHA
JAVA
MACCHIATO

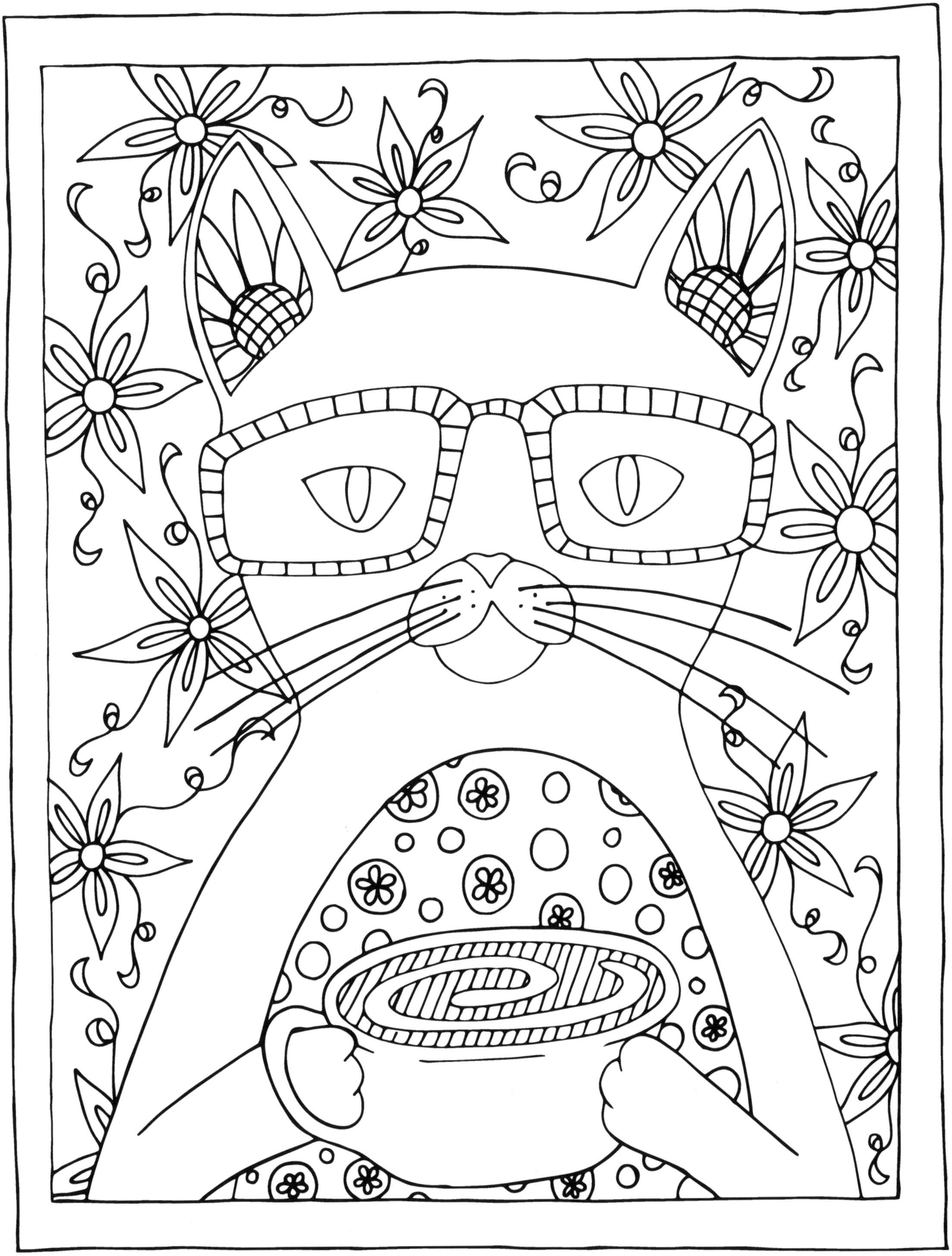

I DRINK COFFEE TO AMPLIFY MY AWESOMENESS

Liquid Love

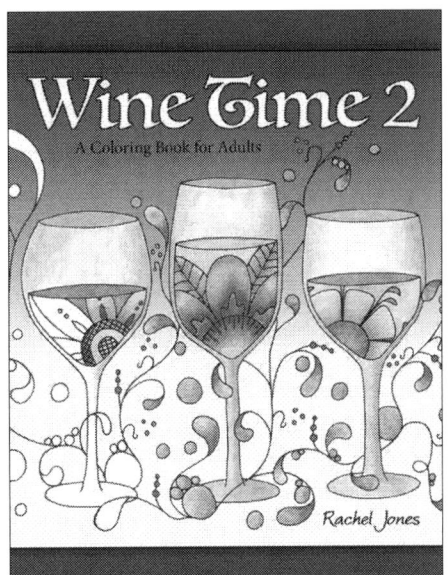

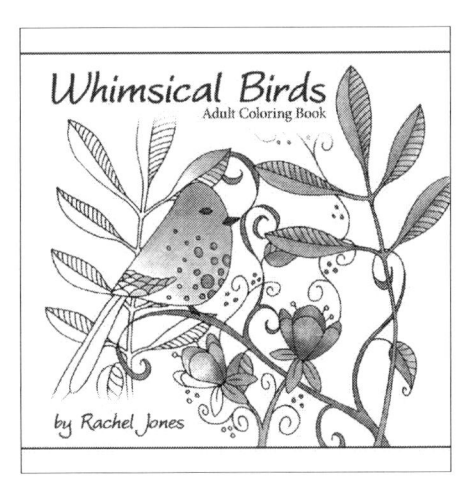

Get more coloring books at RachelJonesArts.com

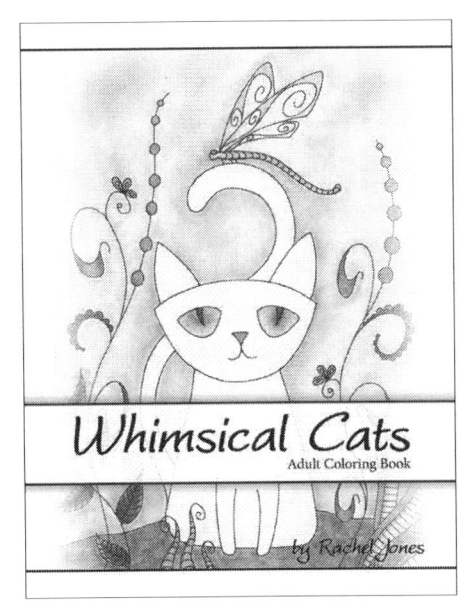

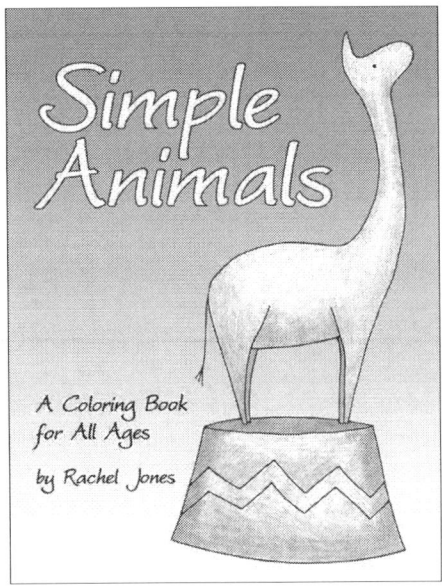

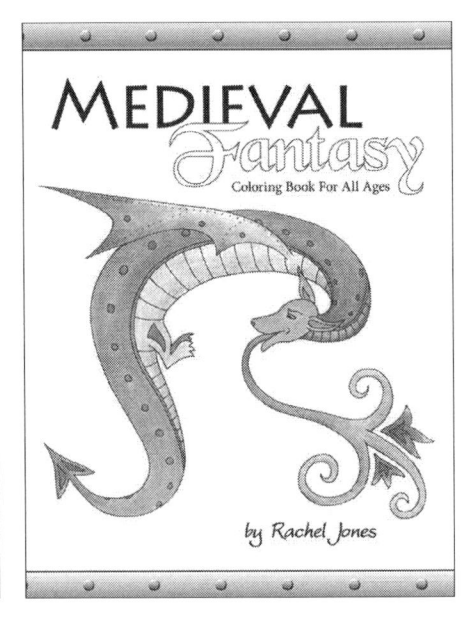

Made in the USA
Lexington, KY
17 February 2019